Exploring

Cannock Chase

by John Roberts

WALKWAYS

by walkers...for walkers

****

WALKWAYS
John Roberts
67 Cliffe Way, Warwick
CV34 5JG   01926 776363
john@walkwaysquercus.co.uk
www.walkwaysquercus.co.uk

****

Exploring
Cannock Chase

by John Roberts

ISBN 0 947708 42 1

First edition 1987 ISBN 0 947708 16 2
Second edition 1993 ISBN 0 947708 28 6

ASSOCIATION OF
FRIENDS OF CANNOCK CHASE

Threats from mining, forestry, gravel digging, the Army and the RAF lead in 1934 to the first group of Friends. Our group started in 1947 with the same aim of protecting the landscape, plants and creatures of the Chase from industry, housing and roads.

We have opposed the M6 crossing over the Chase, helped to map footpaths, commented on County plans, removed stray conifers, laid out deer fodder in hard winters, planted oaks and put up nest boxes. And we have published booklets on the deer and the industrial history of the Chase. Our programme includes walks, talks, photography and hard outdoor work.

The Friends are affiliated to the British Deer Society, Council for the Preservation of Rural England, Staffordshire Wildlife Trust, Staffordshire Industrial Archaeology Society and rambling groups. We talk regularly to the county and district councils, the Forestry Commission and local landowners.

The Friends are a small group who help protect this unique heathland for ordinary people. We are the only independent public voice to advise and protest and we want your support. Please join; contact

**Trevor Warburton, 29 Stonepine Close, Wildwood
Stafford ST17 4QS or 01543 571241**
www.cannockchasedc.gov.uk/caves/focc
iii

Contents

Preface

This book is the successor to my very popular *DaywalkS: Cannock Chase,* published in 1993. That book gave step by step directions to a dense network of interlinked walks covering the whole of the Chase and included a fair bit about the history, geology and so on. It was reprinted four times but it had grown old so I decided to make a complete revision. *Exploring Cannock Chase* will still lead you to nearly every part of the Chase on foot but includes a lot more up to date material on points of interest. It covers recent developments too, such as changes in forestry policy and the campaign to remove acres of unwanted stray conifers to restore the heathland.

John Roberts

Thanks

- to Roger Wilson of Forest Enterprise, Abe Turner and the Forest of Mercia Team, Sue Sheppard of the Saving Cannock Chase project, Debby Smith who knows a lot about squirrels, and the Cannock Chase Rangers. Between them they provided masses of information about the plants and creatures and the present and future management of the Chase.

A special thank you to the Friends of Cannock Chase who gave so much help with my first book. They provided detailed information about the geography, geology, history and industry of the Chase that now forms a large part of this one.

I must also acknowledge the unwitting help of SJ and GP Whitehouse whose books I drew on for the military history of the Chase. *A Town for Four Winters* covers the Army training camps of the First World War whilst *Kitbag Hill* tells the story of RAF Hednesford in World War II.

Essex Bridge

Great Haywood

Stepping Stones

Meet the Chase

What we now call Cannock Chase covers 17,000 acres (26 square miles) of heathland and forest on a kidney shaped plateau above the general level of surrounding Staffordshire.

The Trent Valley to the north and east of the Chase is about 200 feet above sea level; a rough average height for the Chase would be 450 feet. The high points are Stile Cop in the south east at 670 feet, Castle Ring on the southern tip at 780, Rifle Range Corner in the centre at 670 and the Boulder in the north west at 630 feet.

Historically the Chase included the area to the south between Cannock, Burntwood and Brownhills, but the 19th century urbanised and industrialised them so they became quite different from the deserted northern half. The Forest of Mercia project, outlined later, is making great progress towards greening and beautifying this hard worked landscape.

The ground is a sandy gravel dropped by the great glaciers as they melted in a warming climate about 10,000 years ago. Look out over the open heath from say, the Boulder, and you can see how the Chase was made from great heaps of material, dumped as if by monstrous tipper lorries.

If you regard the Chase as one solid block, it is cut through completely only by the deep valley of the tiny Rising Brook between Cannock and Rugeley, which carries the A460 and the railway. The Brook may not look much, but it may have served the world's first blast furnace at Slitting Mill.

The northern third of the Chase has small, steep hills. Three main valleys cut south to north towards the Trent; Sher Brook, Abraham's and Oldacre valleys in order of size. On the rest of the Chase the valleys and streams run east, again to the Trent, the Stoney Brook, Rising Brook and Shropshire Brook. The southern two thirds of the plateau has more massive, domed hills than the north, but they are hardly less steep.

The north-west area has open heath and the oakwood of Brocton Coppice. There is more heathland in pockets around White House, Rifle Range Corner, Brindley Heath, Moors Gorse and Marquis Drive and, as you can read in the feature on Forestry, there is now the prospect of more open ground as some of the felled conifers are not replaced.

The heath areas, which belong to Staffordshire County Council, have heather, bilberry, bracken and silver birch. The rest belongs to the Forestry Commission who have planted mainly Corsican and Scots Pine and manage it as commercial forest. Often the pines are quite majestic and excitingly alpine; in places the blocks are fringed with pleasing fringes of beech. The whole of the Chase proper and some of the outlying fragments, such as Gentleshaw Common to the south, are an Area of Outstanding Natural Beauty, and there are several Sites of Special Scientific Interest.

Fallow, muntjac and red deer wander the Chase and there are badgers, foxes, squirrels, adders and lizards. With the brooks and pools, little green glades, high points and views, rolling sandy hills and pebbly tracks, the Chase offers fine, varied walking, and it is usually dry underfoot.

There are leaflets and maps about every feature of the Chase; its general history, charcoal burning, iron smelting, the First World War Army camps, transport history and the deer. See them at the visitors' centres in Marquis Drive or Birches Valley or at the Museum of Cannock Chase in Hednesford.

Walking the Walks

All the walks begin at one of the seven starting points listed below but you can also pick them up at other places. Walk 2, for example, starts at Milford with paragraph (1) but you could join it at the Boulder and start from paragraph 8.

The walks are all 6 miles long or less, which will not be enough for some people, so you can link them together to make longer circuits.

You can see which walks start from the various places and the further walks you can join from each. This is not all though, because from your added walk you could set out on another, and from that another, so that even long distance walkers can have a good day out. They could walk the perimeter of the Chase (parts of Walks 1,3,6,9,8,7,5,4 and 2) and cover some 25 miles, or they could follow a series of loops and go a lot further. Clear directions show where and how you can switch walks.

Example
Start at Castle Ring and follow **Walk 8** to the Golf Club,
Join **Walk 7** to Moor's Gorse,
Rejoin **Walk 8** via Horsepasture Pools to Castle Ring.

The total length of both walks is 10.5 miles/17 kms but you would cover 8.25 miles/13.5 kms because part of each walk is missed out.

I have not included a complete list of possible walk combinations and distances because it would be long and complicated. You can just assume that when you link walks together you will cover less than the total distance.

Walk directions are separate from the description and set in short, numbered paragraphs in a different typeface.

Distances in yards or miles are to give you a rough idea how far to walk. You do not need to measure because there will be something to look out for, such as a T junction or a brook. So if I say "go .5 mile to the green fence" you will not start to wonder after 200 yards if someone has made off with it. **Distances in paces** are to be counted out.

Half R (or L) means a half turn, or about 45 degrees. **Bear R** (or L) means a narrower angle than a half turn, or just tending away from straight ahead. A **road** has a tarmac surface with a white line down the middle. **Lanes** are tarmac but smaller and without white lines. **Drives** are the same but not public. **Tracks** are wide enough for four wheeled vehicles and might have an earth, grass or stone surface, but not tarmac. **Crosstracks** (one word) are like crossroads. A **path** may have any surface, from mud to tarmac, but is only pedestrian width. The track/path distinction is often hard to make on the Chase where many ways fall between the two.

I don't think you need a compass on these walks because these directions should be clear enough to make sure you don't get lost. You will be fine so long as the directions seem to make sense. If suddenly they don't, go back to the last point at which they did and think again. If you are still confused most probably something has changed and if you can't work it out go back to the start.

The **maps** are sketches to a rough scale of 2.5ins/1 mile or 4cms/1km. The small numbers that appear on them refer to paragraphs in the directions. I have not tried to show buildings or woodland, because there is such a mosaic of patches.

If you want an Ordnance Survey map to help you find starting points and for general interest. Get the Explorer Map 244 (scale 1:25,000: 2.5 ins/mile or 4 cms/km).

The **map symbols** are mainly pretty obvious but here are the main ones.

Starting Point	●	Path	...··..··...··
Track	- - - -	Road, lane, drive	⌒
Railway	+++++	Canal	⌐⊥⊥⌐
Stream/river/lake	～～⊂▷	Car Park	▢
Pub	▲	Trig. Point	△

Amendment Service

The countryside changes all the time. Paths are diverted and hedges removed, there are new tracks, fences and barns. For example, on the Heart of England Way some 15 changes occurred in one period of three years. To keep walk directions up to date I issue Amendment Slips - a unique and **free** service.

Phone or **Email** me (number and address on back of title page) with a note of the books that you have and I will send you up to date Slips. **Even new** or recently purchased books can suffer changes within weeks. (The slips will be available from my website in the near future.)

Please write, phone or email to report any changes or problems, stating book title, walk and paragraph number.

Don't bother copying changes into your book(s). Just dab affected paras with highlighter and keep the Slip in the front pocket of the plastic cover.

Many people never use this service because it's far too much trouble.

The Country Code

* Enjoy the countryside and respect its life and work
* Guard against all risk of fire
* Fasten all gates
* Keep your dogs under close control
* Keep to public paths across farmland
* Use gates and stiles to cross fences, hedges and walls
* Leave livestock, crops and machinery alone
* Take your litter home
* Help to keep water clean
* Protect wildlife, plants and trees
* Take special care on country roads
* Make no unnecessary noise

Beware of the Forest

The conifer woodland on the Chase is managed as a commercial forest to produce crops of timber. From time to time Forest Enterprise send in crews and machines to fell or thin trees or to plant new ones. We have the right to walk through the woods on Public Footpaths and Bridleways of course, and there is also a general permission from the Forestry Commission to walk everywhere else. However, this permission is subject to occasional closures to prevent walkers being nutted by falling trees or mangled in machines.

Warning notices are posted around work sites. A **yellow** one just warns you that there is work going on in the area, a **red** one tells you not to climb on timber stacks while another **red** one says that a certain area is closed and you must not enter. Most often this one does not apply to the tracks people walk on but to the forest on either side. Even so, it may sometimes cover tracks (except Rights of Way), so please cooperate.

Starting Points

Milford

Map reference SJ 976211. A green open space at the junction of the A513 Stafford – Rugeley road with a lane.

Seven Springs

Map reference SK 004205. A picnic place reached by a track opposite a side road off the A513 Stafford – Rugeley road.

Boulder

Map reference SJ 980181. A stonking great rock on a plinth by a trig point which can be reached by a lane from Brocton or from a junction with the Brocton – Pye Green road.

Marquis Drive Centre

Map reference SK 005151. Visitor's Centre reached from minor road between the A460 Cannock – Rugeley road at Hednesford and Flints Corner.

Rifle Range Corner

Map reference SJ 999168. A car park named Penkridge Bank 250 yards east of the road bend marked "Rifle Range Corner" on the minor Penkridge – Rugeley road.

Moors Gorse

Map reference SK 024151. A layby near a waterworks on the A460 Cannock – Rugeley road.

Castle Ring

Map reference SK 045126. Iron Age fort on the southern tip of the Chase just north of Cannock Wood.

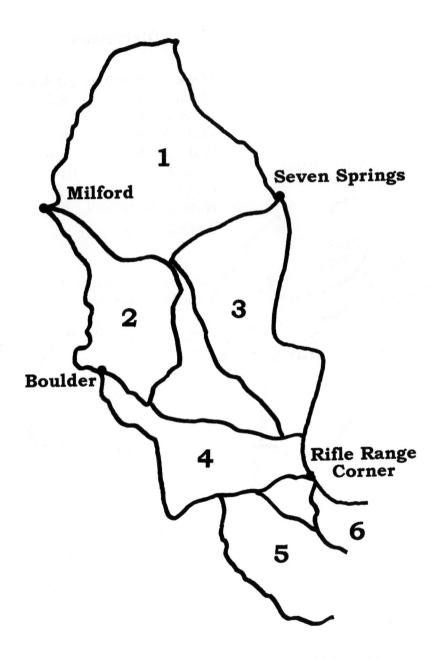

Milford

Seven Springs

1

2

3

Boulder

4

Rifle Range
Corner

6

5

Distances

Walk 1	6 miles	10 kms
Walk 2	5	8.5
Walk 3	6	10
Walk 4	5	8
Walk 5	4	6.5
Walk 6	6	10
Walk 7	5	8
Walk 8	5.5	9
Walk 9	5.5	9

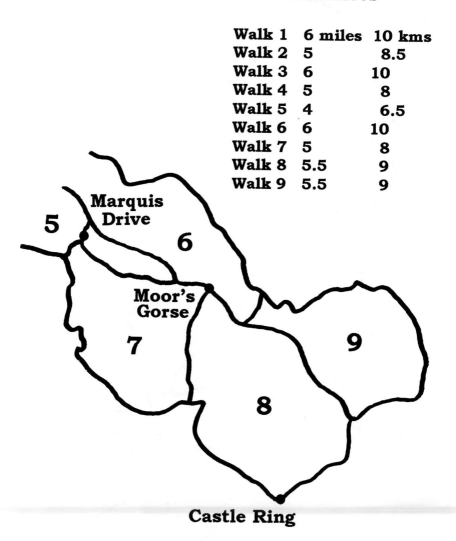

Marquis Drive

5

6

Moor's Gorse

7

9

8

Castle Ring

Shugborough Hall

pool at Milford

**Trig Point near
the Boulder**

Walk 1 - Milford

Starting point: front of the café and Tourist Information hut.
Length: 6 miles/10 kms.
Walks you can join: 3, 2.
Refreshments: Café and Barley Mow at Milford, Lamb &
Flag and Red Lion at Little Haywood.

Rivers, Railways, Canals & Springs

This walk follows the Staffordshire & Worcestershire Canal then
the Thames & Mersey and crosses the River Trent twice and the
Sow once.

The first **railway** is the West Coast Main Line. The deep cutting
and the grand, classical tunnel portico were demanded by the
landowner, the Earl of Anglesey, to protect his Shugborough Hall
from the vulgarities of steam travel. At Great Haywood you meet
the line from Stoke on Trent just before the two lines join.

The **Staffordshire & Worcestershire Canal** starts from
its junction with the **Trent & Mersey** near Great Haywood
and winds south-west to the River Severn. Near the junction the
canal spreads into the broad lake of **Tixall Wide** where the
canal broadens to become a strange lake fringed with bullrushes
and anglers. This was probably the suggestion of Capability Brown
because it was in view from Tixall Hall, now vanished, and its
magnificent Tudor gatehouse, which you can see.

From the lock near the canal junction, step aside to see the
mediaeval Essex **packhorse bridge**, a mellow stone structure
at the meeting of the Rivers Sow and Trent. There is also a cast
iron bridge that carried a private road from **Shugborough
Hall**, famous for its dotty stone follies.

The **Seven Springs** are in the woodland to the left of the car park as you enter, where they form several beautiful pools. The **Stepping Stones** cross the Sher Brook which rises about three miles south at the centre of the Chase.

(1) From front of Café & Tourist Information hut, cross road & go half L across grass to car showroom. CARE. Cross A513 and take side road to T junction.

(2) Go L (Tixall etc) .3 mile (over railway & River Sow) to canal, then take steps down to towpath.

(3) Go R 2 miles, finally crossing aqueduct to meet Trent & Mersey Canal.

(4) Go R 1.25 miles to bridge 72, pass under & turn R up to road.

(5) Go L under railway & over bridge to A513. CARE. Take lane opposite up to car park.

Seven Springs

•••
Option
To join Walk 3 turn to Walk 3 para 1.
•••

(6) Keep to R side of car park & pass pole barrier. Take 1st track R & go 50 yds to 4 way junction.

(7) Go R (past Deer Protection sign) & follow gravel path 1.25 miles to brook with stepping stones.

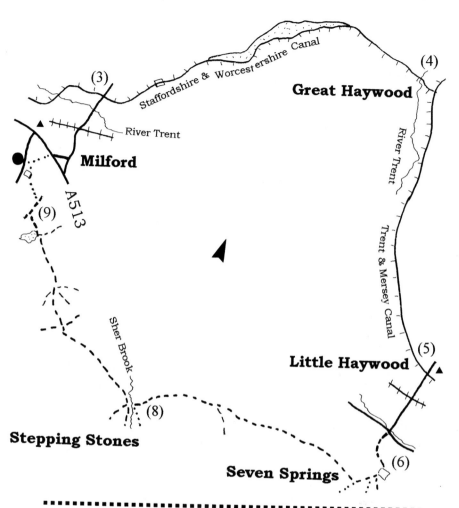

(3)

Staffordshire & Worcestershire Canal

Great Haywood

(4)

River Trent

Milford

River Trent

A513

(9)

Trent & Mersey Canal

Sher Brook

(5)

Little Haywood

(8)

Stepping Stones

(6)

Seven Springs

Option
To join Walk 2 cross stream, turn L & go to Walk
2 para 5 & start from "Keep ahead..".

(8) Cross stones & go R .4 mile to crosstracks.
Take steep path ahead (Milford), cross summit &
crosstracks then drop to pass 1st & 2nd ponds L.

(9) Go R, pass lone pines on your R & curve L
down to car park.

Walk 2 - Milford

Starting point: front of the café and Tourist Information hut.
Length: 5 miles/8.5 kms.
Walks you can join: 3, 4.

A Railway, a Rock
& a Strange Device.

This walk soon joins the Chase's largest visible remnant of World War I, a deep rising **cutting** leading to a curved embankment. This was the formation of the Tackeroo Railway, built by the Army in 1914 to supply the training camps on the Chase.

The cutting also starts the **Heart of England Way** on its 100 mile wander to Bourton on the Water in the Cotswolds. You will see waymarks right across the Chase to Castle Ring, and if you keep walking south you can visit Lichfield, Meriden, Henley in Arden, Alcester, Bidford on Avon and Chipping Campden before you reach the end. I can thoroughly recommend the walk and the brilliant WALKWAYS guide book, and I know what I'm talking about because I wrote it.

The bulrush pool at the head of the old rail cutting is **Mere Pool**. There are sand and gravel quarries on the Chase so this might be one, or it could be due to the peculiar conditions beneath the melting ice sheet. My guess is that the navvies took it out in 1914 to build the embankment.

The walk runs south for some way beside the **Sher Brook**, a small, clear stream that runs from the heathland of the central Chase to the birch and oak woodland on the north-western corner. The valley is so vast that when you consider how the Chase was formed it is more like that the stream occupied the valley than created it.

On the edge of the open heath overlooking the Sherbook Valley stands a massive granite **boulder** weighing about 2.5 tonnes. This area marked the southern limit of the northern ice sheet that carried the boulder from Criffel in southern Scotland.

The western side of this walk follows the edge of the **Oldacre Valley**. It feels very wild and far away, with birch, heather and bilberry but no surfaced track or forest road. The Oldacre Burn rise near the northern end and makes the valley bottom a springy, soggy wetland which is best avoided.

On Broc Hill is a semi circle of rough hewn rocks and an iron plate marked with some squiggles. This is the **Sundial**, and if you stand on the plate in the right position for the current month your shadow will fall onto one of the numbered rocks.

The massive and twisted Scots Pines on Broc Hill are **"Anson's Pines"**, planted in 1780 to commemorated Admiral George Anson's voyage around the world in 1740-44. He was only the second British commander after the Drake to complete the trip and on the way he captured a Spanish treasure galleon, which accounts for his family's grand home at Shugborough Hall.

(1) From front of café & Tourist Information hut, cross road & go half R across grass to car park & ticket machine. Take rising path behind it to meet stone track.

(2) Go L & pass pond L to markpost for Heart of England Way. Take path bearing L to junction of tracks with red/green post.

(3) Follow line of rising cutting (parallel track on its R is nicer), to track junction by post No.5.

17

(4) Take FALLING track L 300 yds to track junction. Go R 700 yds to track junction by stepping stones.

Option

To join Walk 3, cross stream & turn to Walk 3 para 11, but don't go R, go ahead by fence.

(5) DON'T CROSS. Keep ahead with stream on your L for .8 mile (track leaves trees & passes Sabrina Way post) to Staffs Way post, then take track R.

(6) Go 100 yds to junction & fork L. Pass track L & climb to track junction with markpost on crest.

(7) Go L along ridge 450 yds to markpost (Staffs Way & Heart of England Way). Go R to find trig point & glacial boulder.

Boulder

Option

To join Walk 4, turn to Walk 4 para 1.

(8) From boulder go to road & cross to car park. Take path with two markposts & count 118 paces, cross 1st path & take 2nd path R.

(9) Follow small path, winding & sometimes indistinct, down to valley bottom & main track, then turn R.

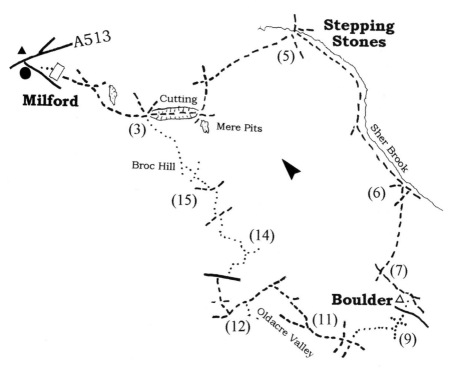

(10) Go down valley 350 yds (at 50 paces cross track junction) & take next path R by reedy pit.

(11) Follow past path L & climb out of valley to join track from R. Keep ahead & join 2nd track from R to markpost.

(12) Count 125 paces & take track R. Follow it 250 yds to lane.

(13) Go R 35 paces & turn L to gates. DON'T ENTER. Go R 30 paces, take path L & cross causeway to far end. DON'T CLIMB AHEAD.

(14) Go L down path & follow to fence corner. Go L 400 yds (cross track, pass green track L, cross track & pass track R) & go down to valley track.

Mere Pits

"Turn L, LOOK at hill ahead.."

(15) Turn L, LOOK at hill ahead & note steep path rising from base. Cross valley towards it & take steep path to crest.

(16) Pass stone thingy close on your R & follow track towards pines, stepping off L to pass between the oldest live trees, & find small path.

(17) Follow path down to track junction with red/green post. Take RISING track R over crest, & bend L. Pass pool on your R, go up between pines & down L to starting point.

Walk 3 - Seven Springs

Starting point: where the drive enters the car park.
Length: 6 miles/10 kms.
Walks you can join: 4, 1, 2.

Three Valleys
& a Trig Point

Left of the car park at Seven Springs is a **wetland** with a many small pools that reaches some 300 yards east to the edge of the Chase. On the adjacent land is a chain of small lakes strung up the valley. All this water comes down the **Old Brook** which is one of the streams of the Chase. None of them are long but they drain a lot of water and of course, they all join the River Trent.

Abraham's valley is a fair example of the two thirds of the Chase that are owned by the **Forestry Commission**. Most of the trees are Scots and Corsican pine with some larch and sitka spruce and there are areas of Norway spruce to feed the Commission's Christmas tree trade. These conifers alone would make for rather a bleak environment but the valley is actually quite beautiful. Self seeded birch softens the woodland edges and green glades; near the water there are alders. The Commission have used beech by the tracks to edge plantations.

The Chase has been heavily **quarried** for sand and gravel and the quarry near Bevin's Birches passed on this walk has made a crater about 1100 yards long and 600 yards wide. There is more about this elsewhere, but this walk drops into an abandoned part of the quarry system and then travels up a long, sandy valley of heather and bilberry. Midway you cross a huge mound of gravel which was once part of a World War I rifle range.

(1) Put your back to car park entrance & go ahead. Pass L of two pole barriers & follow path across grass into trees.

(2) Follow woodland path (becomes stone track) up valley for .6 mile, to pass 1st track L. Go .75 mile & take 2nd track L.

(3) Cross small valley, pass track L & go up to crosstrack. Go ahead 400 yds to wide stone track.

(4) CROSS main track, go R 16 paces then take track L. Go 400 yds to junction with markpost opposite fence corner.

(5) Take small path R down to valley bottom & crosstracks. Go R up BOTTOM of valley 400 yds (over a crosstrack) to fork. Bear R & climb over gravel bank.

(6) Resume path up valley bottom for .4 mile to stone track & markpost.

●●●
Option
To join Walk 4, take track opposite & turn to Walk 4 para 4.
●●●

(7) Go R, cross a track, pass gates R & go 150 yds to track junction. Go R .5 mile & through forest to track junction with trig point L.

(8) Take 2nd track from L & go .6 mile (past L fork), to track junction. Bear half L for 20 paces to 4 way junction, then take rising track ahead.

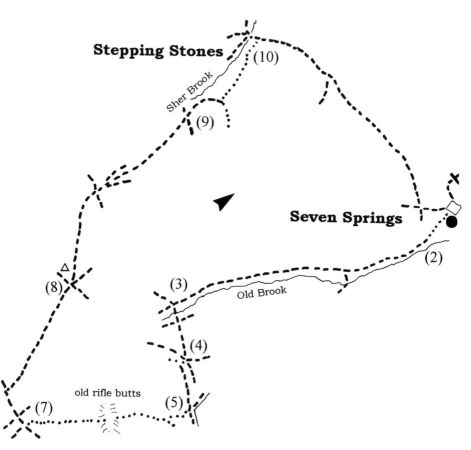

(9) Go .5 mile, eventually falling to track junction in valley bottom.

(10) Take main rising track ahead 200 yds to junction. Go L .3 mile to open picnic area with gate ahead & stepping stones L.

....

Options
To join Walk 1 turn to Walk 1 para 8.
To join Walk 2 cross brook, turn L & go to Walk 2 para 5 starting from "Keep ahead.."
....

(11) Go R by fence 1.25 mile (past R fork) to picnic area, then go L to car park & start.

Walk 4 - Boulder

Starting point: boulder.
Length: 5 miles/8 kms.
Walks you can join: 3, 6, 5, 2.
Refreshments: café at Springslade.

A Spring, a Memorial & a Topograph

Dropping first into the valley to cross the Sher Brook, this walk then climbs away from it only to pass its source later. It crosses the higher ground of Anson's Bank which give good views to the north-west and returns down the quiet and remote Oldacre Valley.

Gospel Place is a remote place at the head of the Sherbrook Valley, with open heath on the west side and forest to the east. The pines heighten the feeling of sandy wilderness. You can see how the Sher Brook gradually forms in a damp patch, though there is nothing to see of the brook except the head of a little valley which promises a stream sometime.

The Brook is the boundary between the parishes of Brocton and Brindley Heath and the name of the place has something to do with beating the bounds on Rogation Day. Perhaps so, but at this spot I can imagine a bearded man in robe and sandals preaching to a multitude.

The **Katyn Memorial** commemorates 14,000 Polish soldiers and professional people murdered in the Katyn Forest in 1940. For some 50 years this mass murder was blamed on the Nazis but conclusive evidence has since shown that it was committed by Soviet forces.

24

The waymarks tell you that this walk follows the **Heart of England Way** across Anson's Bank. See Walk 2 for more on that. There are fine views of rolling Staffordshire where a **topograph** presented by a firm that makes glue will explain what is where. Near the car park at about midway is a leftover from the First World War, a concrete structure which supported a hopper for loading coal wagons on the Tackeroo Railway.

(1) From the boulder, walk away from road onto open heath. Go R to post No. 4 & take track L to post No. 5. Fork L & follow main track .5 mile down into valley to stepping stones.

(2) Cross stream, pass 1st track R & take 2nd (rising) track R. Follow it .6 mile (across 3 way junction & past tracks L, R & L) & go round L bend to steel barrier.

• •
Option
To join Walk 3 take track L & turn to Walk 3 para 7, starting from " ...5 mile.. ".
• •

(3) Go ahead across car park, pass 1st & 2nd steel barriers L, then on 124 paces to markpost, and take track R.

(4) Go 500 yds to car park at

Rifle Range Corner.

• •
Option
To join Walk 6 turn to Walk 6 para 1.
• •

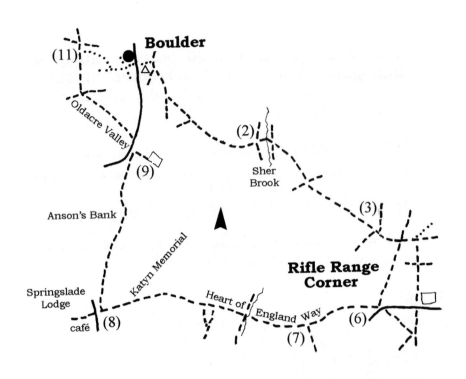

(5) From car park entrance cross road WITH CARE & take track opposite for 150 yds to 3 way junction. Turn sharp R for 300 yds to road bend. GREAT CARE.

(6) Cross road to pole barrier & take track beyond. Go .35 mile to track L by HoEW markpost.

..
Option
To join Walk 5 turn L & go to Walk 5 para 9. **.....**
..

(7) Go on down track 1 mile, crossing valley bottom & rising to road.

(8) Take path R .7 mile (passing R fork, several tracks & topograph at 20 paces L) to meet road at car park entrance.

26

(9) Go ahead down road 80 paces to hump & white posts. Take path L 60 paces to short markpost at 3 way junction & take middle path down VALLEY BOTTOM.

(10) Go .6 mile down to bridleway markpost.

■■
Option
To join Walk 2 turn to Walk 2 para 10.
■■

(11) Take rising path R 500 yds to meet path by post. Go L to road & cross to boulder.

a present from Scotland

WWI remains

Walk 5 - Marquis Drive Centre

Starting point: door of Visitor Centre.
Length: 4 miles/6.5 kms.
Walks you can join: 4.
Refreshments: café at start.

Heath & Forest

Heading west from the Visitor Centre, this walk crosses **Brindley Heath**, site of one of the Great War camps. Although covered in pines until recently, the area never was planted by the Forestry Commission. Some trees were put in by the County Council but a great many were self sown. These trees have now been felled and the ground is being allowed to return to what its name suggests. There are still some conifers before you reach the road but in time they will go. Then the only trees between the northern and southern heath will be the half mile thick belt which you cross next.

On the whole I do not like things set in straight lines, whether it is the design for a book cover or my garden, but for the gravestones in these **cemeteries** they seem right. The steady ranks of stone slabs across the lawns, all the same height, all at the same distance, adds a solemnity which reminds you that each one represents a dead man.

The **open heathland** that follows has never been planted with trees and is the way Brindley Heath will look in the future. This is free and exhilarating country and I want more of it.

The rest of this walk follows the **Heart of England Way,** so at least you have some waymarks to follow. It is all conifer forest but quiet and attractive.

28

(1) From door of Visitor Centre, follow pavement to car park. Walk along its L edge to Scots pine, then go ahead & take grass track.

(2) Pass L fork, go round L bend (past path R), go round R bend (past path L), then round L bend (past path R) to 3 way junction. Go R down path to drive.

(3) Go R to road. CARE. Cross, go L 100 yds & enter car park R. Pass barrier & follow main track 1 mile to road. DON'T CROSS HERE.

(4) Go R along verge 200 yds (past markpost on far side of road) to 2ⁿᵈ post (if still standing). CROSS ROAD WITH CARE & take track opposite.

(5) Go .3 mile to road. GREAT CARE. Cross road bearing L & take small path (crossing earth track) to tarmac drive.

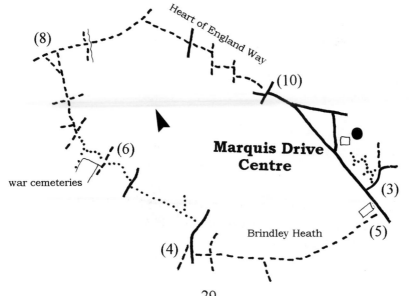

(6) Cross bearing R, take path beside cemetery fence to its corner on edge of open heath, & meet track.

(7) Go R, pass track R & go down. Cross a track, pass track L. Note that track rises then passes 2 tracks L and falls into valley to junction of tracks.

Option

To join Walk 4 go L .5 mile to road & turn to Walk 4 para 8.

----

(8) Go R down to valley, then keep ahead 500 yds to markpost & take track R.

(9) Follow track 400 yds to road. CARE. Cross & take track to T junction. Go R 30 paces & go L to T junction. Go R 35 paces then go L to road.

(10) CARE. Cross road, go ahead across verge & follow road to R bend. Enter drive L, jump ditch R & cross grass diagonally to car park etc.

Walk 6 - Rifle Range Corner

Starting point: car park entrance.
Length: 6 miles/10 kms.
Walks you can join: 9, 8, 7 ,5.
Refreshments: café at Marquis Drive Centre.

Brooks, Lakes & a Camp

From the plateau around Rifle Range Corner this walk drops into the sandy Fairoak Valley then falls a little further to cross the valley of the Rising Brook. This is the main cleft across the Chase which carries the A460 and the railway. Deep, sandy tracks in steep valleys lead you in a half circle to cross the A460 again followed by a long haul up Marquis Drive to the Visitor Centre. Here you are back on the plateau with an easy finish.

The walk down **Fairoak Valley** past the lakes on the Stoney Brook is one of the best on the Chase but other brooks have also been dammed. There is the Old Brook at Seven Springs, the Rising Brook near Moor's Gorse and also at Hednesford and Slitting Mill. The Shropshire Brook is dammed at Beaudesert and the Bentley Brook at Hednesford. There are many other odd little pools with varied vegetation. This is not surprising given the fast draining powers of the Chase sand and gravel, but a full survey of all these water features might be interesting.

The track named **Marquis Drive** was built by the Marquis of Anglesey, one time owner of the Chase, to link his home at Beaudesert with hunting areas in the Sherbrook Valley. During World War II the section between the railway and the Visitor Centre was known in the RAF as **Kitbag Hill**. Trainee aircaft technicians came by rail to a station at Moor's Gorse and had to carry their kit up to the camp. There is more about this in the military section.

31

(1) From car park entrance cross road WITH CARE & take gate opposite. Follow stone track past tracks R & L to cross pole barrier.

(2) Go 550 yds to road. GREAT CARE.

(3) Take track opposite to pole barrier, & join track. Go ahead past houses to T junction.

(4) Go R 100 yds to power pole with gizmo by steel barrier. Leave track & take path L down to crosstracks by pool.

(5) Go L .5 mile (past 3 lakes) to track junction with ford R.

(6) Go R & cross stepping stones. Go ahead .5 mile (past tracks L & R) to road & houses.

(7) Cross & go R on footway. Pass under rail bridge, then cross road & follow footway, bending R to A460. FAST ROAD - GREAT CARE.

(8) Cross & go R down slip road to bottom. Take track L .4 mile to 1st track L.

••
Option
To join Walk 9 turn L & go to Walk 9 para 3. •••••
••

(9) Continue on valley track 500 yds to fork. Take rising track R 150 yds to crosstracks, then go L to main track with HoEW markpost.

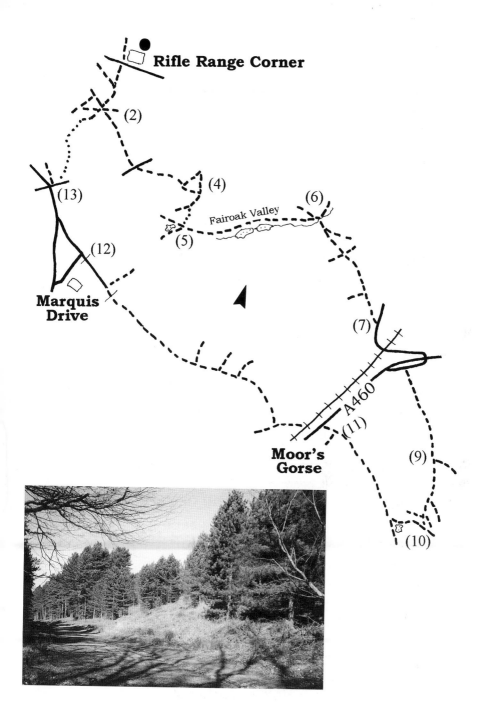

Rifle Range Corner

(2)

(4)

(13)

Fairoak Valley

(6)

(5)

(12)

Marquis Drive

(7)

A460

(11)

Moor's Gorse

(9)

(10)

33

··

Option

To join Walk 8 go R 200 yds, pass pond & take track L, then turn to Walk 8 para 7.
··

(10) Go R .5 mile to A460. GREAT CARE.

Moors Gorse

··

Option

To join Walk 7 turn to Walk 7 para 6.
··

(11) Cross road, take track & cross railway. Go 1.25 miles, eventually passing steel barrier to reach double steel gates.

··

Options

To call at Visitor Centre go L & return to this point.

To join Walk 5 go L to Centre & turn to Walk 5 para 1.

To join Walk 7 go L to Centre & turn to Walk 7 para 1.
··

(12) Go ahead & join road, keeping to R side. Go ahead to near house, then bear R & follow verge path to road. CARE.

(13) Cross road, go R 45 paces & join path L. Follow it to join a track & go 400 yds to junction.

(14) Go ahead through camp site, curving L to join exit track, & cross road to starting point.

Walk 7 – Marquis Drive Centre

Starting Point: door of Visitor centre.
Length: 5 miles/8 kms.
Walks you can join: 8, 9.
Refreshments: cafes at Visitor Centre and Cannock Chase Enterprise Centre.

Remains, Rides & Reservoirs

From the Visitor Centre this walk follows mossy tarmac tracks across a grassy plateau with little glades of silver birch. How strange that the corpse of **RAF Hednesford** should be one of the most beautiful parts of the Chase. It would certainly be better without the tarmac roadways but the cost of getting rid of them in money and damage would be enormous. And they do provide a friendly area for wheelchairs and pushchairs.

Next comes a winding path through mixed broadleaf and conifer **woodland**. The conifers are mainly Scots pine and there is a wide age range, suggesting not systematic Forestry Commission work but self sown trees as on Brindley Heath.

Moors Gorse was the site of the wartime rail halt from where RAF recruits would stagger up Kitbag Hill to the camp.

The woodland to the south is unquestionably **Commission forest** and the only trees you will see for almost a mile will be Scots and Corsican pines. They were planted in the 1970s and 80s so they will be here for some time yet.

The bridleway beside the **golf course** is one of the best walks on the Chase, with open views to the left and the trim greens and fairways on your right.

35

After crossing the A460 for the second time you pass the small industrial estate and public car park on the site of the **West Cannock No.5** pit. Turning north, you walk tracks and roadways that once were part of the works but have been reclaimed for cycling and strolling and nature. Down in the valley to your left a series of pools has been created in the Rising Brook, the oldest of which powered Lord Paget's blast furnaces at Hednesford.

(1) From door of Visitor Centre cross to WC block, pass the front and join a stone track. Cross tarmac path & go on to T junction of paths.

(2) Turn ½ R, cross grass towards car park & meet drive. Go L past pole barrier, follow tarmac drive .4 mile & take green gate.

(3) Go ahead past track L, go round L bend, plus 10 paces, & take earth track R.

(4) Go 65 paces & fork L. Follow path .4 mile down into valley, & meet track.

(5) Go R & cross railway to A460. FAST TRAFFIC.

Moors Gorse.

••
Options
To join Walk 8 cross road & go ahead, then turn to Walk 8 para 6 starting from "... .5 mile."
To join Walk 9 turn to Walk 9 para 1.
••

(6) Cross road & take track opposite. Pass water works & take next track R. Pass steel barrier, pass house R & 2 tracks L to 4 track junction.

(7) Take 2nd track from L & go .7 mile to golf course. Keep ahead past clubhouse to hut.

(8) Pass hut on your R & follow track 1.3 miles to where it bends around a golf tee, then narrows by rusty circular sign.

(9) COUNT 120 paces & take path R. Go with golf course on your R until track levels off at crest. Go L down grass path to meet rough grass track.

(10) Go R 90 paces then turn L down small valley to fence corner. Follow fence around corner to A460. GREAT CARE – FAST TRAFFIC.

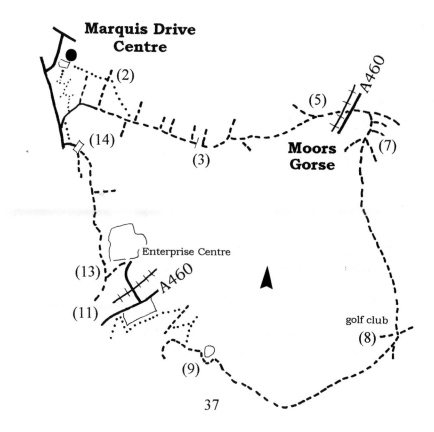

(11) Cross road, go R 200yds & take drive L. Cross railway, curve R up to industrial estate entrance & take path L.

(12) Cross tarmac path & go down to junction with stone tracks.

(13) Go R 450 yds (past L fork) to car park type area. Cross diagonally & follow LEVEL roadway to car park.

(14) From car park entrance follow exit track 50 paces & take small path R. Go 200 yds to driveway.

(15) Go R past car park plus 30 paces, & take path L. Follow to 3 ways junction & turn L. Go round R bend (past faint path L) & at fork go L. Round R bend (past track L) & go up to car park.

two ages of birch

38

Walk 8 – Castle Ring

Starting Point: car park.
Length: 5.5 miles/9 kms.
Walks you can join: 7, 6, 9.
Refreshments: Park Inn at start.

A Fort, a Park, a Pond & a Lake

Castle Ring at a height of about 230 metres is the highest point on the Chase. Walk around the ramparts and the commanding views show why the Iron Age people built their refuge here. Until the mid 1990s the views were negligible, blocked by mature conifers. New forestry policies focusing as much on amenity and natural beauty as on timber growing have meant that after harvesting the trees were not replaced.

The walk skirts the southern edge of **Beaudesert Park** where the woodland is quite mixed, with oak, beech, hazel and shrubby things softening the pines. Take a good look at the pond. Deeper into the trees there are many small depressions, the remains of the pits where coal was mined between the 14th and the 17th centuries. They can sink quite suddenly so keep away and stick to the paths.

After the golf clubhouse the walk follows an old bridleway which falls steeply down to Moors Gorse. Much that follows is a pleasant but unremarkable stroll through the pines until you reach **Horsepasture Pools**. These small lakes were formed by damming the Shropshire Brook that rises only some three quarters of a mile away near the golf club. This shows how much water is carried by these little streams off the Chase. The pools lie in the lowest point of Beaudesert Park at some 130 metres, giving you a climb of 100 metres back to the start. It feels like a lot more.

(1) From car park head for steps & climb to rampart. Walk clockwise 300 yds & take steps L. Cross ditch & take path ahead to path junction. Go L on FALLING track to meet a main track.

(2) Go ahead across main track, then across a path. T take track ahead by post for 200 yds, to junction.

(3) Go R 1 mile (skirting lake) to road. GREAT CARE – DON'T CROSS.

(4) Go L on verge 250 yds till opposite track R, then cross road & follow track up to T junction.

• •
Option
To join Walk 7 turn L, go to Walk 7 para 9 & start from " ..follow.. ".
• •

(5) Go R to crosstrack by golf hut. Go ahead 1.25 miles then descend to join track by house. Go ahead & curve L down to main valley track.

Moors Gorse

• •
Options
To join Walk 6 go L to A460 & turn to Walk 6 para 11.
To join Walk 9 turn to Walk 9 para 1.
• •

(6) Go R .5 mile & take track R by pond.

(7) Follow for .5 mile to join a track, then go L to road. GREAT CARE.

(8) Cross road & enter car park. Go L past steel barrier plus 400 yds to cross a track (with HoEW post). Go ahead .6 mile to T junction.

(9) Go R to iron gates. Go R by railings 100 yds & take earth path L.

(10) Go 200 yds to T junction. Go R 200 yds up to fence.

(11) Go R & stay parallel with line of fence for .5 mile to fence corner. *(Ground can be very wet by fence; you can diverge downhill & return to fence later.)* Pass fence corner & keep ahead to track, then go L to get onto rampart & return to start.

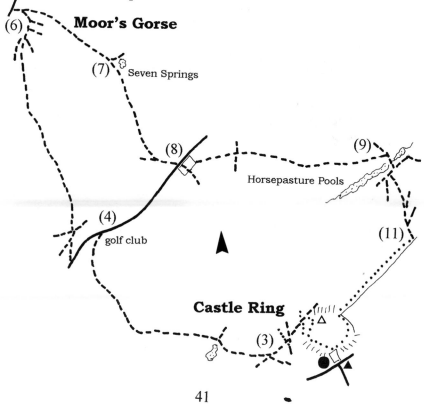

to Upper Longdon

Horsepasture Pools

Walk 9 – Moors Gorse

Starting Point: eastern (non-railway) side of A460.
Length: 5.5 miles/9 kms.
Walks you can join: 8.
Refreshments: Chetwynd Arms at Upper Longdon.

A Trig Point, a Ridge, & a Sandstone Track.

This is the most varied walk in the book. Starting on tracks through the pines, there is a climb of 75 metres in a quarter of a mile to the trig. point at **Stile Cop,** 207 metres. From this high point you can see miles of small hills and the cooling towers of Rugeley power station, if you like that sort of thing. Erotically curved, they have all the grace of well engineered objects, like electricity pylons, but they are always in the wrong place.

The ridge from Stile Cop is sandy **heathland** with tracks and paths through the gorse which lead to a small but spectacular **quarry**. The green pastureland that follows rises to the shoulder of a hill, giving more long views.

A long, sunken track with sandstone walls leads to the quite village of **Upper Longdon** where nothing seems to happen. Another track through the pines takes you on to Horsepasture Pools, which I mentioned in Walk 8. I presume they were created for pleasure by the Earl of Anglesey who for many years owned Beaudesert Park.

After a slight but surprisingly long rise you reach Wandon and join Marquis Drive to pass the old Youth Hostel, now a caravan park, and return to the start.

(1) From non-railway side of A460 take wide main track (Heart of England Way). Go .5 mile, pass track & pond R, then on 250 yds to markpost, & take path L.

(2) Go down to tracks & keep ahead. Pass track R & go on 400 yds to markpost, then take track R.

(3) Go up steeply 500 yds to crest & track junction. Go L & curve R to gate & lane. Take path opposite, pass path L & curve R up to summit & trig point.

(4) Go L down wide path, pass path R & go .5 mile (past track L where track widens & misc tracks) to horseshoe sign. Go on 200yds to track junction.

(5) Go R & immediately pass path L. Go on 350 yds, cross sharp dip & rise but stay on ridge to see quarry R. Walk around its rim then go down into hole, then exit L to road. GREAT CARE.

(6) Cross road, go L along fence to enter gap & cross stile. Follow path to T junction. Go L 130yds to wooden gate L, & take track R to cross stile.

(7) Follow fenced path & cross stile. Go L & cross stile. Go ahead to top fence & cross stile. Keep ahead to crest & cross stile.

(8) Follow R hedge & cross field corner stile. Cross field passing midfield oak close on your R. Keep this line then (when in view) head for R end of tree clump, & join track.

(9) Go L to track junction. Go R .5 mile to road at Upper Longdon. GREAT CARE.

(10) DON'T CROSS HERE. Go R 350 yds to last house R (No. 126). Cross road, cross end of stone track & take stone path.

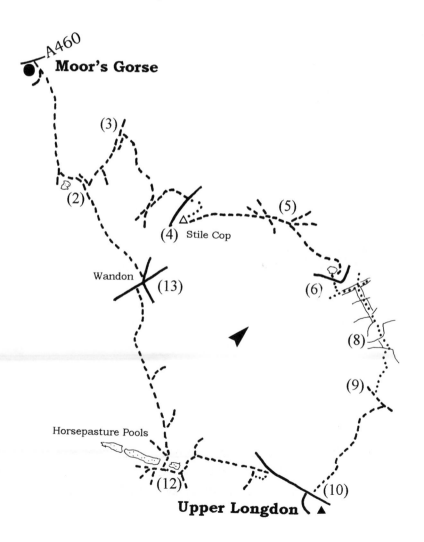

(11) Go 80 yds & meet earth track. Bear R past house, take stone track 450 yds & cross stream, then curve R to iron gates.

■■
Option
To join Walk 8 go ahead by railings 100 yds & take earth path L, turn to Walk 8 para 10.
■■

(12) Go R by railings, pass track L & follow main track .7 mile to road. CARE.

(13) Cross road & go R to junction. Take stone track L & follow it 1.25 mile back to start.

near Stile Cop

46

Man on the Chase

Some 10,000 years ago the last (or latest) ice sheets left the Midlands. Much of South Staffordshire was left covered by a clay that used to be called Keuper Marl but which geologists have lately renamed, with uncommon lack of inspiration, Midland Mudstone. Dull it may be, but things grow in it, which was to made it very different from the pebbly, sandy area to the south of the new River Trent. This hilly plateau was relatively exposed and became covered only by a thin, acid soil which meant that it would never be farmed.

As life became viable in northern regions people moved in, hunters and gatherers slowly learning the techniques and advantages of agriculture and permanent settlement. Flint chippings are the earliest evidence of man on the Chase. In 1910 six hundred specimens including twenty eight tools were found on the site of a Neolithic flint works at Cannock Wood. There is no natural flint to be found near the Chase, but we know that there was a trade in unworked nodules that would be manufactured locally. The two ancient roads that cross the Chase, Blake Street and South (or Sow) Street, were probably used for trading in flints and salt.

With this activity at Cannock Wood we can guess that the nearby high point of Castle Ring was in use from the earliest times. The Iron Age fort may have been built by a powerful tribe who controlled Staffordshire, Shropshire and Cheshire from a capital at Wroxeter. There are five ramparts on the less steep, southern side and one rampart fronting the Chase, all enclosing eight acres. The wide views that the fort commands and the ease with which access could be controlled must have made it easily defensible. The function of these structures is not totally clear. Some may have been used for permanent settlement but others may have been a temporary refuge in times of danger. Small forts on waterless hills seem likely to have been the latter, but there is water in the Ring (at least, there is now) and one can imagine a small village there.

Castle Ring

commanding views

The Romans seem to have kept clear of the Chase, which would have served no strategic military purpose. They passed it by to the south on Watling Street, the modern A5, though there were forts at Wall, just south of the Chase, and Penkridge to the west.

Anglo Saxon tribes entered Staffordshire in the late 700s and like the Britons, probably kept to the lower, more fertile ground. Around the Chase there were Saxon settlements at Bednall, Acton Trussell, Brereton and Armitage.

In the early mediaeval period Staffordshire was the most thinly populated county of England. The Domesday Book of 1086 describes the Chase as waste lands and records no settlements. It was part of the ancient Forest of Cank, which at 54 square miles was the largest woodland mentioned. The Normans extended the original wildwood by plantings to promote deer hunting and applied the draconian Royal Forest laws. By 1286 the Forest boundaries ran from Stafford down the Penk Valley in the west through Wolverhampton, Bilston, Wednesbury, Walsall, Lichfield, Tamworth, Alrewas and Rugeley back to Stafford. It therefore included areas which are still recognisably heath or woodland today, such as Whittington Heath, Druids Heath, Bentley Heath, Barr Beacon, Hints Woods and Hopwas Woods.

The small Cistercian Abbey of St Mary's was founded in 1141 at Radmore, about a mile south of Castle Ring. The monks stayed only 15 years during which they were left the "vill", or lands around, Cannock before moving back to the mother house at Stoneleigh in Warwickshire. The move was prompted, according to one theory, by the more fertile land at Stoneleigh, but the Cistercians were not softies. All their abbeys were set in the most desolate and unfertile regions, such as Strata Florida in Mid Wales and the north Yorkshire Moors. More likely is the suggestion that life on the edge of the Chase was dangerously lawless. When the monks left in 1155 the lands reverted to the Crown.

The Norman (Royal Forest) Chase included nine manors or "hays", Gailey, Teddesley, Ogley, Cheslyn, Bentley, Alrewas, Hopwas, Cannock and Rugeley. The term survives in the modern names of Cheslyn and Ogley Hay. There is also Boney Hay but we are not quite clear how that fits in.

In 1289 Richard I needed to raise cash for his crusade and sold the manors of Cannock and Rugeley to the Bishop of Lichfield and Coventry. They were withdrawn from the Royal Forest and the area became the Bishops Chase, the first reference to the name. He had residences at Beaudesert and Shugborough.

When Henry VIII's dissolved the monasteries their property fell to the Crown and Henry VIII sold the Bishop's land to Sir William Paget, whose descendents became Marquises of Anglesey. They occupied the Bishop's former palace at Beaudesert, which became Beaudesert Hall until it was demolished in 1935. Marquis Drive was built across the Chase to take the family from their home to the hunting in Sherbrook Valley.

Disaforestation, in the legal sense of ceasing to be a Royal Forest subject to Forest Law, continued through Tudor times. Deer Parks were established at Wolseley, Teddesley, Hatherton, Hagley, Beaudesert and Shugborough; the names still appear on the map. In 1560 the Pagets were licensed to fell timber to fuel their iron smelters and foundries, such as those at Furnace Coppice and Slitting Mill near Rugeley. I cover the tale of the Pagets and the destruction of the oakwoods later, but the outcome was that most of the oaks had been cleared before the next century. Grazing sheep cut down any oak seedlings, so preventing the woodland from regenerating, and their numbers and lack of management caused erosion of the thin acid soil, so creating the heathland.

During the next two centuries the Chase was a heathery waste with nothing to exploit, while coal and iron were worked to the south and east. Photographs taken by soldiers training on the Chase in the Great War (1914 - 1918) show a treeless wilderness. In their excellent book on the Army camps, *A Town for Four Winters*, CJ & GD Whitehouse compare the soldiers photographs of various places, only identifiable through great skill and knowledge, with their own pictures of the same. To those urban young men from the bustling industrial cities, the Chase must have seemed barren beyond hope.

heathland near the Boulder

Following the destruction of woodland over centuries, Britain suffered a serious shortage of timber during the Great War. In 1920 the Forestry Commission was created and given a remit to grow a strategic reserve of timber. On their land in the south and east of the Chase they planted the best that the ground would support: Scots and Corsican Pine, with some Lodgepole Pine and Larch. More recently they have put in Sitka Spruce. The close planting of the trees, the monoculture and the regimentation was supported by forestry thinking of the time, which was aimed at maximising timber production. Happily the main aim has now shifted towards amenity, and modern forestry practice sits far better with conserving and enhancing the beauty of the Chase.

Gravel extraction became important between the wars and there are now gigantic craters at Bevins Birches on the east side and Pottal Pool in the south west. Worked out quarries at Brocton and Milford have been left to develop as nature reserves. Chase gravel is the biggest, finest quality and most easily worked supply in Europe. The scale of the danger to the Chase can be imagined if you go and see what has happened at Bevins Birches where there is still an active quarry lease and plans to extend workings towards South Street.

During World War II the RAF ran a training camp at what is now the Marquis Drive Visitor Centre. It was more compact than the Great War camps, but after the war the military still wanted to keep hold of 2,440 acres of the Chase. Certain areas to the east side were still used as firing ranges during the 1990s, but now they seem very little used. In 1950 the Ministry of Transport wanted to run the M6 over the Chase but that proposal was defeated.

Perhaps the repulsion of the M6 was some sort of watershed for the Chase because it marked a period when its fortunes improved. In 1955 the Earl of Lichfield gave some 2000 acres to Staffordshire County Council to be preserved for public access and nature conservation. In 1958 the Chase was designated an Area of Outstanding Natural Beauty and in 1973 four and a half square miles in the north became a Country Park. The Forestry Commission have long had an open access policy to their portions, which is common to all their woodland.

Taken together, these different strands amount to a shift from private to public ownership and a realisation of the idea that public amenity and conserving the environment is important and beneficial to society. English Nature and the Heritage Lottery Fund have backed a five year scheme called Saving Cannock Chase to restore the open heathland and views across the Chase. I deal later with the details, but it's a very bright and positive sign. Even so, watch that quarry.

Slades & Things

Explanations of place names can sometimes be interesting but many turn out to be as mundane as old wellies. Sherbrook is a golden exception. A few remain baffling and we are probably all the better for it.

Beaudesert - beautiful wild place.

Brereton - briar hill.

Brindley Heath - woodland cleared by burning.

Broadhurst Green - a hurst is a hilltop clump of trees and this was a wide one with a clearing.

Dimmings Dale - Demon's Dale??, search me.

Etching Hill - formerly known as Eychilhill 1504, Ichinhill 1584, Iching Hill 1694, Eachings Hill 1798, Hitching Hill 1834. Goodness knows what it means.

Flaxley Green - a woodland clearing where flax was grown.

Gospel Place - on the boundary between the parishes of Brocton and Brindley Heath and named after the Rogation Day ceremony of beating the bounds.

Hagley - wood were haws were found.

... ley - as a name ending means woodland pasture.

Moors Gorse - moor or marshland.

Rising Brook - Ryssinbrooke 1584, a stream with its source in brushwood.

Sherbrook - Sherbroke 1290, the shining stream.

Shoal Hill - Le Sholle 1300, Shore Hill 1834 - a hill with a twisted shape.

Shropshire Brook - it is miles from that county and flows away from it. The name probably comes from of a tenant.

Slade, slad - valley. Hence Deercote Slade – a shelter (cot) for deer. The other slades are obvious - Hazel, Spring etc.

Slitting Mill - a village grew around a mill on the Rising Brook in the 1700s. See the industrial history bit for " slitting".

Stile Cop - steep hill. So it is.

Rocks & Contours

"*Geology of Cannock Chase*" by Paul Green is comprehensive and fascinating. Get the booklet from the Marquis Drive Visitor Centre for 50p and learn all about it. In the meantime, here is my plain person's, homemade and potted account of how the Chase was made.

Deep beneath the Chase lie the layers and layers of ancient rocks which form the earth's crust. We don't really know very much about the deeper regions, but from boreholes, mining and occasional outcrops geologists have been able to form a picture of the surface and what lies beneath to a depth of about 8,000 metres (4.88 miles).

On top of a basement layer of ancient rocks formed between the very birth of the earth and about 440 million years ago lies an undulating layer of limestone formed in the Silurian era. This reaches (so far as traced) from Mid Wales into the Midlands with occasional surface outcrops such as Wenlock Edge. No such rock appears on the Chase and the nearest outcrop is at Wren's Nest in Dudley, but all later rock layers laid upon it reach the surface to affect the form and character of the Chase.

After the Silurian the layers of rock seem to skip 170 million years or so because the next band of rocks is from the Carboniferous period. One layer of rock often sits on another in the "wrong" order but it doesn't mean that nothing happened during the interval. Probably later foldings, tiltings, slippings and erosion of the earth have shifted the missing bit to somewhere else. The Carboniferous started some 345 million years ago, a period of shallow seas and marine and freshwater swaps. Layers (or seams) of coal were formed from decayed vegetation but they were only 3% or so of all the rock of that time, the rest being layers of sandstones, ironstones, mudstones and marl clays. They run northwards at increasing (and unminable) depths but get nearer the surface again under the Potteries. The Chase coal measures slope down to the west, and Littleton Colliery was working beneath the Chase to a depth of some 915 metres (.6 mile).

Like the Silurian rocks, these Carboniferous formations can be traced underground for many miles and particular seams of coal were worked in coalfields far apart. So in North Staffordshire a certain seam was called Ragman. It appeared in the Cannock pits where they called it Benches and further south in the West Midlands it became Thick Heathen. The character of the coals change over such a distance but geologists can still recognise them and the layers of miscellaneous sandstones etc in between.

During the Triassic period 230 million years ago pebble beds were laid down by fast flowing water. They are cemented together into a conglomerate rock and layered with sandstone to a depth of between 30 and 90 metres. Most of the pebbles are a grey-purple quartzite which may have come from what is now northern France, but others are sandstones, volcanic rocks and limestones from south and west England.

In the succeeding 200 million years it is most likely that further layers of rock were formed on top of these, but they are not to be found. The last great climatic event to occur before our own times is the one that left the Chase in its present form, the last ice age.

About 2 million years ago there was a general lowering of temperatures causing snowfields to form in the mountains, followed by ice caps and glaciers. The ice masses increased in size until they formed vast sheets covering most of north-west Europe, and this was the pattern until some 30,000 years ago.

During this big freeze the climate varied slowly all the time. Quite temperate periods might last a few thousand years, when the ice would release meltwaters which flooded out to remould the landscape. Then the temperature would fall again and the ice would advance, with rocks shattering in the cold and the glaciers gouging up debris.

Between 26,000 and 10,000 years ago a bank of ice still covered the Chase and much of Britain to the north. In fact the Chase may have been the tip of a southern salient. The ice was at its most dense some 18,000 years ago before there was another vast shift in the climate.

It is usual to say that the ice retreated. It didn't of course, it melted and dropped all the rock and soil scooped up over millenia in the great grind south. Melt water formed beneath the glaciers and was forced under great pressure to find a way out. Imagine a refrigerated jacuzzi churning with meltwater laced with pebbles and sand, and whirling through ice caves.

The ice dumped boulder clay around the western and southern fringes of the Chase while racing meltwaters formed a series of steep sided valleys, which are now called slades.

The calm and comely contours of the Chase that you see now are the result of later erosion by rain and wind, which has smoothed and sculpted the wild work of the meltwater.

The Chase north of the Beaudesert area is, more or less, covered with glacial deposits lying over the Triassic pebble beds, or mixed up with them. Although nearly 230 million years separate the Triassic from the work of the ice it is pretty well impossible to distinguish pebbles from the two sources. To the south the Carboniferous coal measures are near the surface because, at some stage, this formation was pushed higher and the loosely compacted Triassic layer eroded away. You might expect the boundary between the two areas to be the deep valley of the Rising Brook that carries the main A460 and a railway between Cannock and Rugeley. Actually, that is a glacial valley and the change of surface rock follows the minor road to the south that runs between Brereton and Hazelslade via Wandon and the Golf Club.

If you made a triple decker sandwich with marmalade, peanut butter and sardines, you might cut it in half. If you held the halves so that the marmalade in one was level with the sardines in the other, you would have what geologists call a fault. On the east and west sides of the Chase are the Rugeley and Bushbury faults. They mark the edges of the Chase and beyond them the surface rock is the dismally named Midland mudstone more typical of this part of the Midlands. To the south the Bentley Fault separates the two coalfields, Cannock Chase from South Staffordshire. In fact there are many faults across the southern edge of the Chase but they are underground and do not affect the surface so obviously.

Habitats, Plants & Creatures

There are at least five different types of natural habitat on Cannock Chase. The heathland and the conifer plantations are the most obvious but there is also deciduous woodland, valley wetlands, grassland and what I will call "scrubby heath".

They all provide food and shelter for different plant and creatures so they are all are important, but the **heathland** stands out. All the other types of habitat can be found in many other places throughout the Midlands and all over Britain. It is true that there is other heathland in the western Midlands. Highgate Common is just west of Dudley, the Habberley Valley is north-west of Kidderminster, the Devil's Spittleful to the west of that town and Hartlebury Common looks over Stourport on Severn. Even so, these are small and scattered fragments.

The Chase heathland is not unique in one respect; is has suffered much the same intrusions and degradation as those other areas. Hence the five year rescue operation now under way called "Saving Cannock Chase" which will be followed by a long term management plan. More on this later; let's look first at what we have now.

The team running the rescue project have issued a leaflet offering a "Healthy Heathlands Recipe". The ingredients are:

5 parts fern (usually bracken)   20 parts grasses
1 part bare ground   4 parts herbs
15 parts trees or copses   5 parts scrub
          50 parts heather and bilberry

The method for cooking this dish adds that you will also need an awful lot of dry, sandy ground, which the Chase can supply.

The Chase is mainly covered by loose, free draining, sandy gravel. It acts like a sieve or colander, so soluble plant nutrients get washed out leaving the thin soil dry and infertile.

This is most obvious on the open heath where there you will find pioneer species of acid ground, such as heathers, bracken, bilberry and its relations, the cowberry and crowberry. The Cannock Chase berry is a unique local hybrid. There are tough grasses such as wavy hair grass, bents, fescues and matt grass. Beside the heathland tracks in sunny places are heath bedstraw, tormentil, eyebright, trefoils and speedwell.

heathland above Oldacre Valley

small Horsepasture Pool in winter

Birds include the rare hen harrier and great grey shrike, a few whinchat and linnets and the more ordinary meadow pipits and skylarks. The Chase's most important breeding bird is the nightjar, which nests on open heath with a scatter of birch and pine and where conifers have recently been felled. Although declining, there are more nightjars on the Chase than anywhere else in the Midlands. The Forestry Commission have cut a lot of timber in the last few years and some of it will not be replanted. I describe this and other aspects of the new approach to forestry in a later feature, but it will be very helpful to the heathland.

The dry, heathy character of the open Chase has been modified in some places where it shelters very different plants and creatures. On Brocton Hill and Brindley Heath disturbance by the training camps in the First and Second World Wars has left what I have called **scrubby heath**, with hawthorn, gorse, brambles, rosebay, nettles and thistles.

The **deciduous woodland** of birch, oak and rowan near Seven Springs and Sycamore Hill makes a more fertile and sheltered environment. All the woods have hawthorn, elder, crab apple and holly. Brocton Coppice on the north-east side of the Chase is a craggily romantic, sessile oakwood with some trees over 350 years old. Today there are also a great many birches, an intrusive but short lived tree.

Early 19th century maps suggest a pure oakwood, and when the Chase was grazed by cattle and sheep new young birch and oak alike would be nibbled back. When the grazing stopped the fast growing birch were able to tap minerals out of reach of the heather roots, so their decaying leaves returned these nutrients to the soil to benefit the oaks.

To help Brocton Coppice into the future efforts have been made to encourage new oaks. In the winter of 1978 acorns from the Coppice were sown in 1 metre square cages. Some had a 3cm mesh while others were smaller. The larger size excluded deer, birds and squirrels and the small mesh stopped mice. More recently local children were encouraged to join a scheme to regenerate the wood.

The old oaks are full of holes offering nesting places for birds and homes for all sorts off beetles and creepy things which live off dead wood, including the death watch beetle.

The tawny owl breeds in the bigger holes. In summer warblers take advantage of the different conditions. The garden warbler usually nests in thick cover such as brambles, as does the chiffchaff. The willow warbler and wood warblers nest more or less on the ground.

Birds in the mixed woodlands include the expected blackbirds, thrushes, magpies, jays and tits. Look out for the long tailed tit which builds a neat hanging nest. All three woodpecker species nest on the Chase. You can recognise the green woodpecker by its "yaffle" call but are most likely to see it in the open. The great spotted woodpecker makes a loud "chick" call when flying. The lesser spotted woodpecker is sparrow sized and only likely to be spotted [sorry] by experienced bird watchers.

Bats love old trees and Leister's, long eared, noctule, pipestrelle and whiskered bats have all been recorded. Forest Enterprise have made great efforts to attract them into the conifers too. The pines have few holes so a huge number of bat boxes have been fitted with some success.

These old woods on the Chase are home to three kinds of reptile, the adder, the common lizard and slow worms. The Chase is probably the adder's main stronghold in Staffordshire.

You may never see any of these creatures because they rush off when they feel the vibrations of human footsteps.

Beech on the Chase has usually been planted around blocks of conifers to beautify the edges. They do not grow to the giant size that you might find on alkaline soils but they do relieve the starkness of the pines. Beech also shelters a rich community of insects and birds, such as the pied flycatcher, redstart and wood warbler and here you will find fungi with off-putting names such as sickener, funnel chartarelle and the highy toxic fly agaric.

Valley wetlands lie near the brooks, in the moist bottoms of some streamless valleys and in some slightly boggy places on the level, such as near the military cemeteries.

There is alder woodland along the Sher Brook, Shropshire Brook, and Stoney Brook. These are good places to look out for birds like finches and siskins in winter when flocks descend on the alders to feed on the cones. From time to time great spotted woodpeckers nest on these trees and the wet conditions underfoot are good for woodcock, which nest on the ground using their dappled brown markings as camouflage. Alder used to be coppiced to create duck coverts, and trees once managed in this way can be found at Haywood Park between the northern stepping stones and Hartshill (Walks 1 & 2).

Peat has developed in the Sherbrook and Oldacre Valleys, so we can add to the Chase flora marsh plants like crossleaved heath, bog asphodel, sundews and marsh violet. In Sherbrook Valley a big tussock sedge grows close to the water. Birds in this habitat are siskins, redpolls and the tits

The poorest habitat on the Chase is in the **conifer plantations**, which consist mainly of Scots and Corsican pine though there is quite a range of others which I mention in the section on Forestry. It must be said that if you have to plant conifers then these two species are well suited to the site and don't look too bad, but they present two main problems.

The first is that neither of these pines is native to the area so they provide relatively poor habitat for the local creatures. Addressing this problem is a matter of long term forestry policies and practice, but in the later feature on forestry you may find that there are now reasons for feeling optimistic.

The other problem is that for many years the young trees were planted very close together. There were sound forestry reasons for this but conservationists complained that it excluded light so that nothing could grow under the trees. In addition, conifer needles are slow to break down and when they do they form an acidic matt, and so the forest floor is pretty well sterile, with virtually no plants, no birds and no insects.

By the time the trees are reaching maturity and have been thinned out several times the woods begin to open up and can become quite pleasant. They still drop acid needles though, which still form a matt, so in spite of the new light, the plants that will grow beneath them are relatively few. Again, policies and attitudes have shifted a lot in recent years.

To be quite fair to the pines, they do attract some birds, such as crossbills, coal tits, goldcrests, tawny and long eared owls and an uncommon bird of prey, the hobby. The pines can also claim one great virtue - they support red squirrels. In the early 1990s small numbers were found on the Chase and nowhere else in the Midlands. They now seem to have disappeared, but for that sad story see the section on squirrels.

wetland..

heath..

and conifers

Forestry

During the First World War Britain found itself desperately short of timber at a time when importing anything was hazardous. In 1919 the Forestry Commission was formed with a mission to secure the future supply of home grown timber, and in 1923 it began planting over about two thirds of the Chase. Today there are almost 7,000 acres of trees giving the Chase a 40% level of tree cover, 34% higher than for the rest of Staffordshire.

The good forester plants the species of trees most likely to achieve his aim, usually growing timber, on the ground and conditions he has to work with. On the mean, dry, acidic soil of the Chase the plantations have been largely Scots and Corsican pine with smaller areas of Japanese larch, Hybrid larch, and lodgepole pine. There are also small pockets of Norway and Sitka spruce.

Corsican pine does best and Chase grown trees give the highest quality timber for structural carpentry, such as roof components and floor joists. Increasingly it is being grown in preference to Scots pine and this has an incidental benefit for the current "Saving Cannock Chase" project; see that section. One of the threats to the heathland has been seed from Commission plantations spreading onto the heathland and growing into unwanted trees. Of the two pines Corsican pine colonises much less than Scots.

Over the years the Commission has increasingly addressed non forestry issues. Most forests have been open for public access, with visitor centres, nature trails and cycle tracks. There have long been sanctuary areas for deer, bats, badgers, grass snakes and other creatures. Planting schemes have put broadleaved trees on the edges of forest tracks, rides and along streamsides.

On the Chase beech was the usual choice for dryer areas, though this native of chalk downland is not best suited to the Chase. The Commission also planted native oak and red oak in selected places. This North American import grows faster and more rangy than native oaks and produces a useful crop of good timber, but the main reason for planting it is its sensational autumn colouring. The Commission have planted sycamore in places, birch quite widely and alder in wetter areas.

The Forestry Commission did not ignore the beauty of the Chase but their main purpose was to grow timber, and Cannock Forest has been very productive. In 1958 when only the earliest plantations had started to mature, 340 tonnes of timber were extracted. By 1965 this had increased to 4,920 tonnes. Twenty years later, production was around 15,000 tonnes a year.

One thing people noticed was that the young trees were planted very close together. This causes dense shade which reduces weeds and the number of knots in the wood, because lower branches get no light, and so die and fall off. The alternative would be hand chopping (brashing) which is expensive. Close planting has certain costs. One is that it encourages lanky trees with little girth that are vulnerable to wind throw. In the section on *Habitats etc* I described the environment beneath close planted conifers.

Early Commission practice was to plant trees at intervals of 4 feet, or 1.2 metres. These days the distance is likely fall between 1.7 and 1.85 metres, depending on the likely future value of sawlogs. Here girth is the aim and is best obtained by giving the trees space, balanced by the need to grow knot free timber.

In 1998 the Gorvernment published *A New Focus for England's Woodlands* which announced the biggest single shift in forestry policy since the Commission was formed. It listed many things

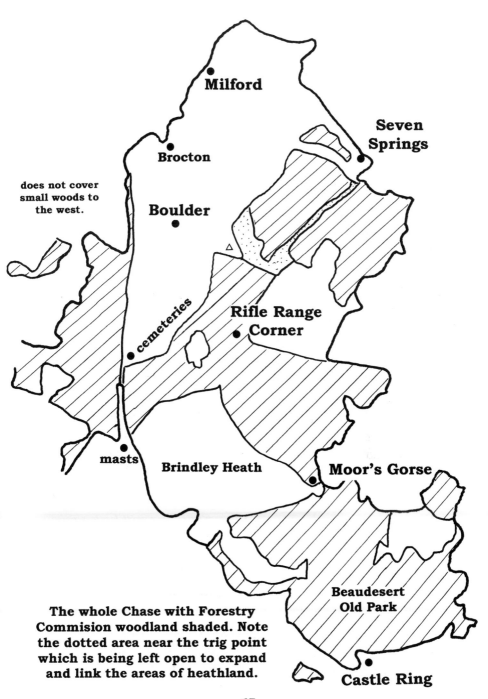

Milford

Seven Springs

Brocton

does not cover
small woods to
the west.

Boulder

△

cemeteries

Rifle Range
Corner

masts

Brindley Heath

Moor's Gorse

Beaudesert
Old Park

The whole Chase with Forestry
Commision woodland shaded. Note
the dotted area near the trig point
which is being left open to expand
and link the areas of heathland.

Castle Ring

that woodland could be used for, such as growing timber, reclaiming derelict industrial land, creating jobs, education, cutting pollution, recreation, enriching wildlife habitat, beautifying the countryside and improving urban and rural environments. Then it declared, in effect, that the new policy was for woodland to do all of these things. Timber growing is still an aim but must be pursued alongside the other aims in such a way that they do not get in each other's way.

The meaning of all this for the Chase is that Forest Enterprise will in future manage their two thirds of the Chase less for timber than for amenity, and for the benefit of the plants and creatures of the Chase, including two legged ones. For example, their Birches Valley centre has a classroom where rangers give talks, and the visitors include some 12,000 children each year.

The effects can be seen in the plans. Cannock Forest is divided into eleven districts, such as Beaudesert and Rawnsley Hills, and for each there are two maps. One called "Future Species" shows how plots will be managed over the next 50 years. Many will be planted with timber trees such as Corsican pine, but the maps show many areas marked as permanent open space, native broadleaved trees, valley streamsides and recreation areas, all non forestry uses. Some areas are already managed in these ways but many will be expanded and many will be new.

Notes about particular sites include, *"This area will be kept open to allow views from the..car park"* – referring to a gap in the Bednall Belt of conifers on the west side of the Stafford road. Then at the head of the Sherbrook valley is an area marked, *"This...area...will be managed as permanent heathland ..."* to create a wide swath through the forest connecting heath to the north and the south. Walkers and cyclists know that the East Trig Point has been standing in a corner of the forest with open heath before it. Again, a swath will being cut through the forest and

"...will be managed as open heathland [to] form a substantial corridor between core areas of ..." heathland.

Many more broadleaved trees are to be planted, though oak in preference to beech. After felling, valleys will remain unplanted and beside many rides and tracks trees will be kept back between 2 and 15 metres from the edges to create a network of open space. The overall effect will be to turn between 10% and 15% of the Forest over to heathland, other areas will be opened out as connecting corridors and there will be a great increase in the numbers of native trees, most of them not grown for timber.

So when will all this happen? It has already started. A few years ago the area just below Castle Ring was thick with pines. Now it has been clear felled and will remain open to give us the same long views as the builders of the Iron Age Fort. Areas near the East Trig Point have been opened up. From Penkridge Bank an open corridor about 100 metres wide will run south into the Fairoak Valley and then up to Marquis Drive, with the trees now growing there scheduled for felling before 2011. These improvements will happen gradually in small packets. The plans for future felling show plots to be harvested year by year, depending on when they were planted, up to and after 2041. The Chase is still growing timber and will go on doing so.

"Saving Cannock Chase"

This five year project aims to restore the open heathland of the Chase by clearing scrub and stray pines and thinning areas of birch woodland. By regular cutting, bracken will be controlled and the heather improved to make the whole area more attractive to a wider range of plants and creatures. Staffordshire County Council, English Nature and the Heritage Lottery Fund are putting £725,500 into the work, which started in 2,000. Pick up the leaflets describing the scheme from the Marquis Drive Visitor Centre.

The particular geology and history of Cannock Chase, which you can read about in other features, meant that in the 17th century it became heathland. Left to itself, the Chase would not have stayed that way.

Leave any piece of land to itself and things start to happen. Old spores in the ground sprout seedlings, birds, animals and the wind bring new seeds. Grasses and shrubby plants grow first followed by small trees and bushes. New wildlife finds a place and droppings, tiny corpses and decaying plants enrich the soil. Quite soon the area becomes a thicket. You can see quite a good model of what might happen on the Chase if you visit Hopwas Hays about 4½ miles south-east of Lichfield.   In time the seedlings of taller trees grow to saplings and thrust up from this shrubby nursery. They grow tall and spread branches until their crowns shade sun and rain from the woodland floor. Light loving plants are replaced by shade dwellers. In time the tall trees die of disease, lightning strike or old age and crash to earth, flooding the wood with light to begin a new and different cycle of plants and creatures. The details of the process will vary according the fertility and climate of the land, but it is always essentially the same.

The people living on and around the Chase interrupted this process. Quite unconsciously, they "managed" the Chase by the simple things they did to get a living. Grazing sheep nibbled away new tree shoots. Bracken was cut for animal bedding, mulching plants, fertilizing the ground and the potash rich ashes were used in glassmaking. Heather was used for animal feed and to make brooms. For fuel they cut turf and felled any trees that might have grown. Thus the villagers systematically cut back plants which would have taken the Chase to its next stage of development.

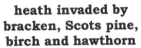

heath invaded by
bracken, Scots pine,
birch and hawthorn

A map of 1775 shows Cannock Heath as extending from Milford, the present northern point determined by the River Trent, to Aldridge just north of Walsall and including Sutton Coldfield. Agriculture, mining and settlements have since reduced this area of heathland to what you see today.

At the same time the towns and new industries provided work and new ways of earning a living, so the traditional bracken and heather cutting died out. For a period the Chase was managed for grouse shooting and the vegetation was kept low to suit these birds. The real threat to the heathland came after the Second World War when all of these uses had stopped. Heather grew big and scrubby, bracken spread uncontrolled, birch and pine colonised wherever their seed landed. Without some form of management to do the work of the sheep and the local people or the grouse shooters, what is left of the heathland will disappear.

Heathland is a scarce environment throughout Britain and internationally. "Saving Cannock Chase" comes none too soon and should go a long way to restoring the Chase. But it is only a five year scheme and the money being spent on it will not be available into the future. What comes next?

The County Council and the Countryside Agency are preparing a long term management plan to cater for everything which affects the Cannock Chase Area of Outstanding Natural Beauty. It will provide policies for recreation, information, nearby road building and development, the future of forestry and the farming that occurs around the edges of the public area, for protection of historic features and for liaison between all interested bodies and groups. And most of all it will provide for the long term maintenance of the heathland landscape.

How can we replace what the villagers and gamekeepers did? Well machines can do some of it but so can animals, so you are likely to see cattle, sheep and possibly horses on the Chase.

Squirrels

When I published my last Cannock Chase book in 1993 there were still some of the native red squirrels on the Chase. No longer. You can't miss the grey squirrels, of course. There are a lot of them and they do great damage to trees. Introduced from North America in the 19th century, they are a pest and have to be trapped. Sadly, the native red squirrel is so scarce in Britain that it can't even be a nuisance. A few hang on in conifer plantations, but this population will not expand without help. They now live only in the north and west of Britain with isolated groups in East Anglia and on some islands.

Many theories have been offered to explain the decline of the red squirrel. Where grey squirrels are present the reds retreat to the conifers, but where there are none reds still occupy both broadleaf and conifer woodland, so the cause seems to be competition. Grey squirrels evolved in the mixed broadleaf and conifer woodland of North America and reds largely in European conifer forests. In broadleaves greys can reach ten times the population that reds can achieve in the same areas, so it seems the grey squirrel is better adapted to live in our woodland. They will eat conifer seeds and they do live in mixed woodland, but they do not do so well in purely conifer woods. In addition, red squirrels suffer mass mortality from the parapox virus, which does not affect greys. Some people have suggested that the spread of the grey squirrel would have been limited had pine martens been more widespread.

Efforts have been made to conserve the Cannock Chase population but helping red squirrels is never easy. For a start they are rarely seen and usually have to be detected from hairs left in sticky tunnels, which are baited to tempt them to enter.

In 1993 a Cannock Chase Red Squirrel project was started with support from the Forestry Commission, English Nature and Staffordshire Wildlife Trust to identify where the remaining squirrels were, how they lived and how they might be helped to increase. Some squirrels were detected but in very small numbers.

This project came too late because there have been no records of red squirrels on the Chase since 1995. This does not mean for certain that they are extinct on the Chase, but the prospects look bleak. We know that red squirrels prefer Scots to Corsican pine because they produce cones at an earlier age and so make a better seed source. Unfortunately Corsican pine is better adapted to conditions of the Chase and is the tree most often planted. Strangely, Cannock Chase reds still exist in Dorset. Some years ago some were sent to Furzey Island off Poole Harbour where they are flourishing in the absence of greys.

There might be some hope for the future of the red squirrel through the "Red Alert" project being run by the Northumberland Wildlife Trust. You can get details from them at Garden House, St Nicholas Park, Gosforth NE3 3XT   (0191 284 6884 – www. wildlifetrust.org.uk/northumberland/RedAlert

Red Alert is focused on identifying areas which might be suitable as reserves for the red squirrel and which could be managed for their benefit. These must be areas of continuous woodland covering at least 200 hectares which are assessed under four criteria: (1) The extent of the threat from grey squirrels, (2) Suitability of the woodland – lots of conifers and very few broadleaves on which grey squirrels can live, (3) Prospects of keeping the area free of grey squirrels - a large area of conifers with no connected broadleaved woodland which is surrounded by a buffer zone of fen or moorland would be best, (4) The attitude of the wood's owners to such a conservation project and whether present and future management of the woodland would fit in with it.

There are things which to some extent favour Cannock Chase. It was the last stronghold of the red squirrel in the Midlands and must therefore be the least unsuitable site. Also, there is a large area of conifer woodland with a useful heathland buffer zone on the western side.

Against the Chase is the presence in many places of patches of broadleaved woodland and of grey squirrels. Could 200 hectares of conifers be found which is surrounded by other conifers to sufficient depth to form a buffer zone? Past experience suggests that we should not be hopeful.

How strange that the only feasible approach to saving the native red squirrel cuts right across current thinking on managing woodland for wildlife. For years conservationists have been urging removal of conifers and planting of native species of broadleaved trees over most of Britain.

[Very many thanks to Debby Smith of Stafford, squirrel expert extraordinary, for her help with this feature.]

The Deer

People like large mammals, so although the Chase has foxes and badgers, rabbits, stoats and weasels, voles and shrews, woodmice, squirrels, adders, slow worms, grass snakes and lizards, what most visitors watch for are the deer.

Marquis Drive Visitor Centre has an exhibition section on the deer. Here you can learn to recognise them and make your own slot (hoof) marks in a sand pit. Look out for the bracket like marks - ( ) - in any soft ground. The Centre also stocks some useful booklets, particularly the authoritative *The Deer of Cannock Chase,* published by the Friends of Cannock Chase.

Deer are browsers that eat, in season, tree shoots, grasses, fungi, acorns and chestnuts, brambles, gorse and heather. If they find themselves in arable fields or gardens they are quite partial to cereals and root crops, peas, beans and carrots. The habitat offered by the Chase is not ideal for them and can support only a limited population, so their numbers are limited by the amount of food available in the harsher winter months. To maintain the population to balanced levels at these times Forest Enterprise has established feeding lawns where food can be left.

Even so, given a mild winter and the deer on the Chase can start to outgrow their food supply. At one time wolves kept the population in check by picking off the weakest and so ensuring its survival and quality. But the last British wolf was killed about 300 years ago, and with no other natural predator, control has depended on the cruelty of starvation or human marksmen. Collisions with cars kill a fair number of deer but they hit strong and weak deer indiscriminately. A skilled ranger who can shoot selected quarry cleanly is by far the most humane control. The exposed position of the Chase makes the deer hardy but not of the best quality, and the winter population is estimated at 400.

Deer roam freely over the whole Chase but the largest numbers are found in the 500 acre reserve area of Wolseley Park. This covers the north-eastern edge of the Chase east of South (or Sow) Street, and has no public footpaths.

Six species of deer are found in Britain but only three of them are native - red deer, fallow and roe. Muntjac deer originate from India and China, Sika deer came from Japan and the sixth species is the Chinese Water Deer. On the Chase we have red, fallow, and muntjac deer.

Red deer is the largest species with the stags reaching 122cm to the shoulder. Like all deer, the males but not the hinds grow antlers annually. Each year they get progressively larger and are cast in March or April. There are probably no more than 50 red deer on the Chase and you are most likely to see them in the southern area where they make mud wallows.

Fallow deer roam wild over the whole Chase, sometimes as many as 600. Most fallow are chestnut brown with white spots in summer but become greyer and less spotted in winter. There is also a pale version. Mixed with them will be the black variety which are dusky brown in winter and sometimes white fallow, which vary in colour from sandy to cream. Bucks grow to about a metre high at the shoulder and have "palmate" antlers, a long wing shape with spikes, very different from a red stag. Fallow have long white tails with a thick black stripe.

Muntjac were introduced into Woburn Park, Bedfordshire during the 19th century but, no bigger than a dog, they soon slipped out into the fields and hedgerows and spread across the county. Gradually they colonised most woodlands in the south and midlands and were first seen on the Chase in 1962. You will be lucky to see them because they rarely grow bigger than 70 cm at the shoulder and can hide in bracken or a bramble patch.

They are red-brown in colour and seem rather hunch backed. The bucks' antlers reach only about 10cm. Muntjac live in small, family groups and can breed all the year round.

On most visits to the Chase I have seen some fallow deer and sometimes red, but I have never seen muntjac. Be watchful, tread softly, and here are two warnings. (1) **NEVER** touch a lone fawn. It has not been abandoned but it will be if you interfere. (2) **Drive carefully** by day or night. Deer can break out yards in front of your car and each year eighty or so are killed by traffic.

Wood, Iron & Coal

Records from the year 1231 mention iron smelting, casting and forging around Rugeley. By 1300 there was an iron mine and in 1472 a forge was set up at Hednesford.

The old method of smelting iron was to heat the ore in an open hearth with charcoal to produce an impure, spongy blob of iron which was reheated and consolidated by hammering. It was a long process which produced indifferent iron, but it required little capital. By 1550 the superior "indirect", or blast furnace, method came into use.

William Paget, lawyer and statesman, was a close advisor of Henry VIII, Edward VI and Mary and he was knighted in 1544. Dissolution of the monasteries in 1537 had made large areas of desirable land available to Henry. In 1546 Paget bought the Beaudesert Estate, covering most of the Chase, and in 1549 he became Baron Paget of Beaudesert.

As Roman Catholics and political figures living in turbulent times, life would not run smoothly for the Pagets, and in 1551 the 1st Baron was sent to the Tower. He returned to favour in 1553 but on the accession of protestant Elizabeth I in 1558 he decided to retire from public life.

Local ironstone, limestone, timber for charcoal and streams to provide water power made the Chase an ideal place for an iron works. In 1561 Paget built a furnace near Hednesford.

High grade iron ore was brought from open cast mines at Walsall, mixed with charcoal and limestone and fed into a twenty foot high brick tower. Three pools formed by damming the Rising Brook powered bellows which blew air into the base of the tower, raising the temperature to 1400 degrees so that molten iron flowed out of the base. The Pagets later established a second furnace at Teddesley and in 1584 the two produced 164 tons of iron.

Rolling and slitting of iron bars to make nails, chains and other hardware was carried on from about 1623 and became the main industry of the area until the mid 1800's. This explains the name of the village of Slitting Mill, with its big, square pool and two waterfalls to provide power.

The charcoal smelting process demanded a great deal of timber and the Pagets started to cut acres of oakwoods. But as Catholics in a protestant state they were suspect, and in 1587 Thomas Paget, the 3rd Baron, was implicated in the Throckmorton Plot to kill Elizabeth I and put Mary back on the throne. The Crown seized the land and in 1589 leased it for a low rent to Fulke Greville, a rascally favourite of Elizabeth I.

Greville savaged the Chase. On the waste that was left there would be no more charcoal, no firewood and no building timber. In the teeth of bitter criticism and a national inquiry Greville went on felling until the end of his lease. It did him no long term harm. He continued with his post as Secretary for Wales, served as Treasurer to the Navy and was Chancellor of the Exchequer from 1614 to 1622. In 1621 he became the first Baron Brooke and was endowed with Warwick Castle. You may be pleased to learn that he was murdered in 1628.

But why didn't they use all that coal? Coal mining was recorded at Beaudesert and Cannock Wood as early as 1298. There were "bell pits" for shallow seams and their remains can be seen at Beaudesert and Brindley Heath. Open cast methods were used in some places, and in others drifts, in which tunnels were driven into a hillside. Sadly for the oak trees of Cannock Chase, all attempts to use coal for smelting were unsuccessful until the process invented by Abraham Darby at Ironbridge in the mid 1700s. By 1757 coke smelting had replaced charcoal.

The Cannock Chase Coalfield lies to the north of the Bentley Fault where the ground is geologically faulty and difficult to work. Richer, easier seams in the South Staffs field produced cheaper coal and the Chase mines could not complete. During the 1600s the surface mine bell pits at Beaudesert were replaced by deeper workings, but with weak technology and poor transport, these efforts were concentrated on the more exposed coal around Rugeley and Brereton.

In time though, the South Staffs fields began to decline and attention was turned to the Cannock Chase reserves. The first deep mine was the Uxbridge Colliery which opened in 1852 working at depths of 800 to 1600 feet. Many other pits followed and eventually totalled 22, using 33 shafts. In 1914 the Cannock Chase Coalfield produced more than both the North Staffs and South Staffs fields.

Only two of these pits were on the area we now think of as Cannock Chase. The Fairoak Colliery opened at Stoney Brook Pools in 1872. It proved very difficult to work and was later transferred to a hill above Dimmin's Dale. For those who know the Chase, the tramway serving Fairoak ran along what is now the main track from Stoney Brook to Smart's Buildings and was later diverted to the pit on the hill. The last pit on the Chase Coalfield was the Littleton at Huntington which closed in 1993.

The pits tunnelled for miles underground and on the southern part of the Chase you will see some memorials to the history of mining. Gloomy little yellow notices warn you to stay on the path because the ground might sink under your feet. However, they refer to the old bell pits which are dotted all over the Beaudesert area, rather than the deep mines.

**the wheel from
West Cannock
No. 5 pit**

**last remains of
RAF Hednesford**

81

The Camps

Between the autumn of 1914 and mid 1915 the Army organised a railway, three miles of road, ten miles of sewerage and water pipes, immense lengths of electricity lines and wooden huts for two infantry divisions with their artillery. Planned for about 23,000 men and 5,500 horses, there were stores, cookhouses, messrooms, stables, canteens, guardrooms and indoor ranges. Later came a post office, a cinema, a hospital, banks and a W H Smiths.

A Town for Four Winters by CJ & GP Whitehouse describes the Great War Army camps. *Kitbag Hill* by CJ Whitehouse is the story of RAF Hednesford from 1938. Both books are admirably researched and amply illustrated with maps and photos. Get them from the Marquis Drive Visitor Centre together with the Staffs County Council leaflet about the Chase in the Great War, which has a useful sketch map.

There were two Great War camps. Brocton sat along the ridge between the Oldacre and Sherbrook valleys with a detached portion on Ansons Bank. Rugeley Camp was around what we now call Rifle Range Corner and the hospital was alone on Brindley Heath.

The camps gave basic infantry training in scouting, PT, signalling and shooting but there never were two complete divisions. They housed reserve and training units and sometimes active units in transit.

The New Zealand Rifle Brigade ("The Dinks") spent time on the Chase, and built a concrete scale model of the Messines Ridges, site of a successful allied attack in 1917. Its gorse covered remains lie a few yards west of Walk (2), where the railway track reached the start of the cutting down to Milford.

German prisoners of war were installed as the war drew on. They were guarded with the usual dismal apparatus of wire and watch towers which were manned by wounded British soldiers unfit for combat. Later the POWs were sent out to work on local farms. The remains of an escape tunnel was discovered after the war but no escapes were ever recorded.

In 1915 the Chase was as raw and treeless as it had been for two centuries. An infantryman wrote home "This is a horrible place on top of a hill ... The cold is dreadful and always a wind blowing and dust flying". Even allowing for the natural bleakness of old amateur black and white photographs, the pictures show depressing ranks of wooden and tin huts with lonely telegraph wires stretching away into a grey fog.

RAF Hednesford, or "No 6 School of Technical Training", was not built on the site of the Great War camps. They had gone twenty years before with sewers choked and hut bases and roads under conifers. In 1938 it was cheaper to build a new camp on the plateau above Moors Gorse with extra housing for instructors at Pye Green and Penkridge Bank. There were to be 800 staff, and up to 4,000 trainees.

Arrivals came by rail from Rugeley or Hednesford to Moors Gorse, where a platform was called Brindley Halt. Then they hauled their kit up Marquis Drive to the camp, and so it became Kitbag Hill.

The camp ran courses for flight mechanics and riggers. Some 81,000 men passed through and under a different title it continued until December 1956. Ten days later the huts were in use as an emergency home for 1,200 Hungarian refugees.

The Chase made another contribution to the Second World War in that tanks built at the English Electric works in Stafford were tested on the western edge. They made a nasty and long lasting mess of the Oldacre Valley.

The camps are now lumps of lost concrete, ditches and ramps, odd patches of cracked and mossy tarmac, ridges of sand yielding copper bullet cases with splatters of lead, and ghostly floorplans of buildings in the rosebay. To see what there is, carry the Great War leaflet as you walk.

The Tackeroo Railway

In 1915 the Army built a railway to supply the Brocton and Rugeley training camps. Staffordshire County Council's *Great War* leaflet (from the Marquis Drive Visitor Centre) shows most of the layout but misses two important parts.

The single standard gauge track left the Cannock to Rugeley rail line at Hednesford just south of the Enterprise Centre industrial estate, once West Cannock No 5 pit. Running uphill beside the road to just south of Nine Gate, it then swung west towards the cemeteries. Originally the line followed the road to the top of Penkridge Bank at Rifle Range Corner, but the steep gradient demanded an extra, or banking, engine. The realignment was made after some trucks ran away and were smashed.

A branch and loop ran east to Rugeley Camp around Rifle Range Corner. The main line continued north past the cemeteries where a branch forked off to run by the west side of the Stafford road to Spring Slade. The main line passed east of Spring Slade and over Anson's Bank to the Glacial Boulder. Here were various loops and sidings. The track ran on along the ridge to pass the modern car park on Coppice Hill and down the long bank to Milford. It crossed the Stafford - Rugeley road (A513) and the lane to Tixall to join the London & North Western Railway's main Trent Valley line.

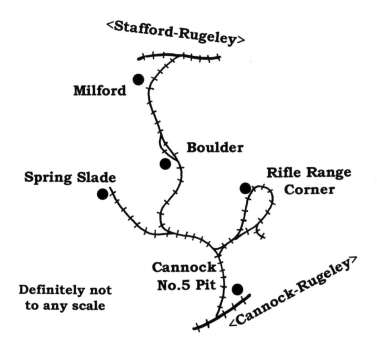

<Stafford-Rugeley>

Milford

Boulder

Spring Slade

Rifle Range Corner

Cannock No.5 Pit

Definitely not to any scale

<Cannock-Rugeley>

You will find odd platforms and concrete structures for loading close to the line of the old track, but there was only one significant piece of engineering. The deep cutting from Milford to Mere Pool is known locally as the "German Cutting", though there were no Germans about when it was built.

Tackeroo was the name of a row of houses just north from Hednesford at the foot of Brindley Valley by the southern end of the camp railway. The inhabitants were said to be surly, short tempered and violent and to have sold watercress and bilberries from the valley, but none of this explains the name. There may be a connection with "truck", or payment of workers in tokens rather than coin, or with "tick", credit. Truck was outlawed in 1835 but decades later some people still called pay day, "truckaroo". On Walk (6) you pass the Forestry Commission's Tackeroo Caravan Site, which is close to Rifle Range Corner on the site of one of the Ordnance Stores with the camp Post Office and two YMCA's nearby.

The Military Cemeteries

At Broadhurst Green on the Cannock - Stafford road there are now Commonwealth and German cemeteries. From 1916 a single burial ground held the victims of illness and accidents in the camps. Many had died in the deadly Spannish Influenza epidemic of 1918 and relatively few were war casualties. The graves are mainly those of New Zealanders and Germans, since most of the British could be taken home for burial.

In 1960 it was decided to rebury here all Germans who had died in various parts of Britain in both wars, and German students prepared a new plot. But the Great War dead were left where they lay, British, New Zealanders and Germans together.

In 1973 the custom of an annual service on ANZAC Day (25th April) was revived here. It is now organised by the Royal British Legion and people come from all over Britain and the world.

About half a mile north at Spring Slade is a newer, more shocking, memorial with no graves. On a slate pediment is a stone inscribed,

"In memorial to the 14,000 members of the Polish armed forces and professional classes who were executed in the Katyn Forest, nineteen hundred and forty (1940)".

For some fifty years this mass murder was blamed on the Nazis but the opening of Russian archives has produced conclusive evidence that it was committed by Soviet forces.

The clean, windy Chase with its heath and pine forests, its sad and tangled history and military past seems a fitting place to remember.

**the Katyn Memorial
and its setting (Walk 4)**

IN MEMORIAM
TO THE 14,000 MEMBERS
OF THE POLISH ARMED FORCES
AND PROFESSIONAL CLASSES
WHO WERE EXECUTED
IN KATYN FOREST
NINETEEN HUNDRED AND FORTY (1940)

The Forest of Mercia

Heavy industry south of the present day Chase has obscured the fact that even in the late 18th century this area was also heath and woodland. It can't be changed back, but the Forest of Mercia scheme is an attempt to reclaim the land for nature and the local people. It covers 92 square miles from the Chase to north Birmingham, and from Wolverhampton to Lichfield, which is, more or less, the area of the old Forest of Cannock excluding the Chase.

This is one of twelve "community forests" started in the late 1980s by the Countryside Commission (now Agency) and the Forestry Commission. Working with County and District Councils, local Wildlife Trusts, The Woodland Trust and community groups, millions of trees planted over old industrial sites, around rundown urban fringes and poor farmland will beautify the environment, give recreation and help cut pollution.

There is no question of thousands of acres of land being planted with dense ranks of conifers. These forests will be more like the medieval Royal Forests that were tracts of countryside with a patchwork of villages, farms, heath and mixed woodland. The idea is that the councils use their powers and influence to plant trees whenever and wherever they can. No one is compelled to sell any land or to do anything, but the councils follow a planting policy with their own land and encourage other landowners to do so with grants and advice. They plant in public parks and open spaces, on old pit sites, around factories, on derelict land, beside canals, in the grounds of schools and on roadsides. Farmers are encouraged to plant in odd corners. New housing and industrial schemes can be made to include the planting of as many trees as possible.

Many small schemes form part of the Forest. Pipe Hall Farm covering 119 acres between Burntwood and Lichfield was bought by the Woodland Trust, planted with native broadleaved trees and opened to the public. Shoal Hill near Huntington is a reclaimed and planted industrial site. Then there are Pelsall North Common, Barr Beacon, Hay Head Wood in Walsall, Chasewater and Hatherton Reservoirs, Hednesford Hills, Gentleshaw Common, and Brownhills Common. Plant liberally with new trees and add many more small woods, parks and nature reserves, all linked by tree lined canals, old tracks and disused railways, and you begin to see a well wooded area

The forest will increase tree cover in south Staffordshire to 30%. Farming, manufacturing, building, travelling and plain living, will go on as before, but there will be more trees and more places to walk, ride, fish, cycle, camp, have picnics or just mess about.

There are walks all over the Forest of Mercia and some of them are linked to the Chase. Most are gentle strolls of a mile or so around nature reserves and country parks, but there are three longer ones; see below. All the walks will in time form part of the "Routes and Leaves" series, a collection of colourful cards describing the walks. Buy the special binder costing (in 2003) £10 (P&P £2), and new cards will be sent to you free as they are published. You can get them from The Innovation Centre, Chasewater Country Park, Pool Road, nr Brownhills WS8 7NL, phone 01543 370737 or forest.of.mercia@staffordshire.gov.uk.

The **Beacon Way** runs for 17 miles from Gentleshaw Common (where it meets the Heart of England Way) to Sandwell Country Park. It visits Chasewater, Brownhills Common, Goscote Valley, Park Lime Pits, Hayhead Wood, Barr Beacon and Merrion's Wood. The trail crosses heathland, pasture and woodland on field paths, dirt tracks, old railway lines and canals, a rewarding mixture of town and country.

The **Forest of Mercia Way** is a fairly new 11½ mile route that I have not yet walked. The northern end is at a junction of bridleways near the masts at Pye Green, that is, nowhere in particular. Running south, it passes through Huntington, skirts Shoal Hill, visits Hatherton and Cheslyn Hay then joins the Wyreley and Essington Canal almost to its end, finally skirting the interesting Rough Wood to end – well, actually, nowhere in particular just north of Bentley. This might well be an interesting and enjoyable walk but I wish it started and ended somewhere. Best of all, such trails should connect with other trails.

The 10 mile **Timberland Trail** opened on 14th March 2003 is a more compact affair in a figure of eight. From Pelsall North Common it traces footpaths over some of the open land around Pelsall and Little Wyrley and part of the Wyrely & Essington Canal. At the opening ceremony we walked a small section and the trail seems a good example of making the best of your local assets through places which will soon see some new trees.

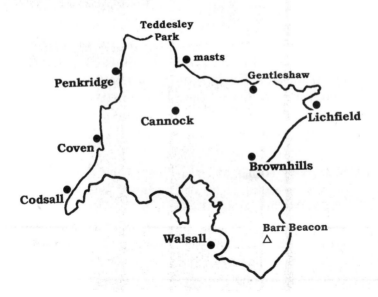

River Sow meets River Trent at Essex Bridge (Walk 1)

Seven Springs (Walks 1&3)

Sher Brook (Walk 2)

**Anson's Pines,
Oat Hill**

**The End
(by kind permission
of Zoe Roberts)**